LIFE-CHANGING
LEADERSHIP

Making a Difference in the Lives of Others

LIFE-CHANGING LEADERSHIP

Making a Difference in the Lives of Others

MIKE BLAYLOCK

© 2007 by Mike Blaylock

All Rights Reserved. No part of this book may be reproduced in any form without permission in writing from the author, except in the case of brief quotations embodied in critical articles or reviews.

Cover design by Susie Simmons

ISBN – 978-1-4303-1843-9

Printed in the United States of America

To my wife Sonja:
You are the inspiration behind all I am and all I do.
I love you!

Table of Contents

Real Purpose	1
Enthusiasm	5
How Do You Get Passion?	9
Express Genuine Interest	11
Pay Attention	13
Learn to Listen	17
Invest Yourself in the Lives of Others	19
Sacrifice	21
Put Others First	25
Motivate with Encouragement	27
Demonstrate Character	33
Give Away Credit	35
Express Appreciation	39
Take Chances on People	41
Be Accessible	43

Empower for Success	45
Remove the Obstacles	47
Go All the Way to the Dorm	49
Fuel Dreams	53
See the Big Picture	57
How Do You Get Perspective?	65
Prevent People Problems	71
Learn to Inspire	75
Focus on What Is Important	79
Epilogue	81

Real Purpose

There is a little cemetery in central Arkansas where several generations of my wife's family are buried. It's near the town of Marshall, and it's called Canaan Cemetery. There are no famous people buried there, but there are folks living in the nearby hills who can tell you about many of the people whose names appear on the markers. However, a lot of the graves in that old cemetery contain the remains of people who have been long forgotten-- people who lived their entire lives and no memory remains except the faded stone that marks their final resting place.

I don't know about you—I want my life to make a difference. Only I am not so concerned about an epitaph on a tombstone in a quiet field. I want my epitaph to be written on the hearts of those whose lives I have impacted. I want to be someone who influences others.

Recently, I have had meetings with several different successful businessmen who have all said to me, "I wish I could do what you do. I just can't seem to find any satisfying purpose in what I do." Each of them were thankful for their jobs, but wanted something more fulfilling. Have you ever felt that way about your job? Do you lack purpose in what you do?

The truth is there is purpose to be found in whatever you do. It involves making a difference in the lives of those who work for and with you. It is about real influence. It is called life-changing leadership.

I firmly believe that influence is the highest level of human ability. It is the difference between just having the title "parent" and actually molding a life. It is that which differentiates between imparting information and really teaching. It is the difference between being someone's boss and shaping the possibilities of a future leader. It is the distinction between taking up space and really making your life count. Meaningful influence brings validation to our lives.

Leadership is all about others. Life-changing leadership is about helping others succeed. It is making a meaningful impact in someone else's life.

How do you become a person of influence? How do you lead with life-changing leadership?

Over the years I have observed many leaders. A few had a significant impact in my life. Sadly, far too many were bad examples. Still, they taught me valuable lessons about leadership.

What are the characteristics of a life-changing leader? What does it take to make a difference?

Enthusiasm

The word enthusiasm originally came from two words, "en" and "theos," literally meaning "possessed by God." It is the picture of being supernaturally charged up. When I think of enthusiasm, I think of preachers and coaches. Both, as a general rule, are possessed with an unusual amount of enthusiasm. Picture that preacher pounding the pulpit or the coach delivering a stirring half-time speech that leads the team to victory. It is that kind of enthusiasm you must possess if you are to influence others.

Oliver Wendell Holmes once said, "Some people die with the music still inside of them."

Passionate people, enthusiastic people, live their lives with the music on the outside! They are excited about life and they are passionate about what they do.

The great high wire artist, Karl Walenda, when asked about his job said, "Being on the tightrope is living—everything else is waiting." If you can have this kind of enthusiasm about the people around you, it is a key part of what will make you a person of influence.

The first of my children to play basketball was my daughter, Ashley. She started playing in the fifth grade and played through her seventh-grade year. The games were rarely high-scoring or fast-paced, but they provided some of my favorite sports memories. In spite of the fact that Ashley wasn't very big and didn't score often, watching her was always the highlight of the game. The best moments were when she would play what I called her "bumblebee" defense. She would get right up in the face of the player she was guarding and wave her arms wildly. Sometimes her arms moved so fast, they were just a blur. There is no doubt in my mind that if a bumblebee played basketball, it would play like Ashley. She never quit, never let up, and her arms never slowed down. Her all-out style was always distracting to the opposing player and often resulted in a turnover. What I loved most was seeing her play all-out. She was full of enthusiasm and passion.

When you want to influence people, you have to have passion for them. They must know that you care about them. They must know that you are fired up about them. That is key in making a difference in someone's life.

I have a great job! I get to hang out with college students. I love college students! I love where they are in their lives. I love spending time with them and helping to mold and shape them. I love seeing them grow and develop. I love seeing them succeed. I love everything about college students. The best part of it is, because I work at a university, I get paid to do what I love. That passion and enthusiasm gives me a great platform for influence in the students' lives.

I have a great passion for the people who work on my staff at the University of Mobile. I love seeing them come up with ideas and create and develop things. I love watching them succeed, and I am absolutely committed to do everything I can to help them be successful. They know they can count on me to be in their corner. That gives me a great platform for influence in their lives.

How Do You Get Passion?

If you don't have passion, how do you get it? It is really very simple. You first must be able to see the potential in others.

I have a very good friend who is a scout for a major league baseball team. His job is to discover potential talent. He has to be able to look at young baseball players, see beyond their weaknesses, and spot undeveloped potential. He sees them as they can be. That is our job. If we are to be influencers, we have to look at others and see their potential.

Once when I was in elementary school I convinced my mom and dad to let me plant a garden in the back yard. I remember going to the hardware store and looking at all of the packages of seeds that were available. There were carrots, radishes, squash, celery and okra, to name a few. I couldn't believe how many different things I could grow in my garden. In my mind, each of those packages was full of real food that my family and I would feast upon. They were packages of potential. That's what the people around you are--packages of seeds that contain endless possibilities for producing fruit. Your job as a life-changing leader is to take those possibilities and make them a reality.

Where do you start?

Express Genuine Interest

Making a difference begins with being genuinely interested in people. It is caring about them and demonstrating that care by being interested in their world.

When I was in college, I attended a church not too far from the campus. The pastor was full of energy and enthusiasm, and he took an interest in me. He would notice when I was gone and call to check up on me. He would take me out to lunch, and we would chat and talk about what was going on in my life. He would even drop by the campus every once in a while and look me up.

I remember one time when I first began my speaking career; I was doing the program for a

Rotary Club. I looked up and saw him slip in the back door. He had come to hear me speak and to support me. He gained a tremendous platform for influence in my life simply because he expressed genuine interest in me. I could tell he really cared about me. That made all the difference in the world.

I was up in Kansas City about a year ago and I went by to see him. He is still at that same church, only now it's the largest church in the state of Missouri. There are around 7,500 people who attend every week. I thought I would never get in to see him. However, some things never change. He rearranged his schedule, took the time and sat down and focused on me. He listened, we talked, and we had the best time. He is a great influencer of people, me being one of them.

Pay Attention

One of the ways to express genuine interest is simply to pay a little attention to people. When I walk across campus at the University of Mobile, or even when I go from one end of the building to the other, I try to speak to everyone who passes me. Sometimes it is just to say "Hi" or "How's it going?" Some people get really freaked out because they are not expecting anyone to speak to them. They are surprised that anyone notices them. Try this the next time you go to the shopping mall. Speak to everyone you pass. I hope you won't get arrested on some kind of insanity charge!

Sometimes people just need to be noticed. They need to feel like somebody knows they are alive.

That is the power of the interested boss or the power of the interested teacher. WOW! I can think back in my life to the teachers who took a personal interest in me. They had a great platform for influence in my life. The life-changing leader is the teacher who teaches students, not subjects. It is the boss who leads people, not employees.

You want to express interest? Ask questions.

- Where were you born?
- What's your favorite ice cream?
- What do you like to do?
- What's your definition of success?
- What is your biggest dream?

The more you know, the better. Find out about birthdays and special occasions. I keep a list of birthdays entered into my PDA. It pops up on my screen a few days in advance to remind me. I will send a card, make a phone call, or in some cases just remember to say, "Happy Birthday" when I see the person. It is amazing that something as simple as remembering a birthday just blows people away.

Get to know the people who work for you. It is important to know and remember things about their lives and the lives of their families. It shows that you really care.

Learn to Listen

Don't you just hate it when you carry on a conversation with someone and you know that they are not listening to you; they are only waiting to talk again. Listening is a powerful part of communication. It not only says, "I care about you" but listening gives you tremendous insight into the person's life that will help you impact them. When someone talks to you, look them in the eyes and give them your attention.

A number of years ago I had the opportunity to interview for a job with a very well-known leader.

I had never met him but I had followed him over the years on television and radio and had read several of his books. After entering his office, he came out from behind his desk and sat in a chair next to mine. For the next hour I had his complete attention. He listened intently to what I said to him. He asked me questions based on things I said to him. At one point when his secretary interrupted with the announcement of an important call, he asked her to take a message and continued to give me his complete attention. This well-known leader showed me the value of giving someone your attention. He made me feel important because he listened to me.

Invest Yourself in the Lives of Others

A number of years ago, my friend Ray Hildebrand came by my house to see me. Ray had a few hit records in the 60s as Paul of the group Paul and Paula. He walked in the front door and asked, "Where is your guitar?"

"It is in the other room," I replied.

"I need to take it," he said.

I asked him why and he said, "I am working with a guy at the penitentiary that needs a guitar, and I am going to give him yours."

He picked up my guitar and headed to his car. I chased behind him all the way arguing, "You can't give away my guitar. I have some concerts coming up and I need it."

I couldn't part with my guitar because I didn't have another one, plus I had spent about $300 on it. He opened the car door, put my guitar in the back seat, and walked around to the trunk. He reached in and pulled out another guitar and said, "I have two of these, so I am giving you this one." It was a Martin D-18 guitar worth about $2,000. I still have it. Ray Hildebrand believed in me and he invested a $2,000 guitar (and much more) in my life. I can honestly say that no single human being has had a stronger impact in my life than Ray. You may not have a $2,000 guitar to invest in someone, but you can invest your life in others!

Investing yourself involves more than just being a mentor—it is pouring your life into the lives of others. It is being committed to help them be the best they can be. It takes time. It takes energy. It takes sacrifice.

Sacrifice

A well-known major league baseball player answered the doorbell at his home one morning to find a very young boy from his neighborhood who asked, "Can you come out and play catch?"

This big-time superstar wound up going out in the yard many times just to play catch with a neighbor boy. He had plenty of other things he could have been doing—but he was willing to sacrifice his time for the sake of a small boy. If you are to make a difference in the lives of others, you need to invest yourself in the lives of others—and that takes sacrifice.

There is an excerpt from Margery Williams' *The Velveteen Rabbit*, which explains what sacrifice is all about.

"What is REAL?" asked the Rabbit one day, when they were lying side by side near the nursery fender, before Nana came to tidy the room. "Does it mean having things that buzz inside you and a stick-out handle?"

"Real isn't how you are made," said the Skin Horse. "It's a thing that happens to you. When a child loves you for a long, long time, not just to play with, but REALLY loves you, then you become Real."

"Does it hurt?" asked the Rabbit.

"Sometimes," said the Skin Horse, for he was always truthful. "When you are Real you don't mind being hurt."

"Does it happen all at once, like being wound up," he asked, "or bit by bit?"

"It doesn't happen all at once," said the Skin Horse. "You become. It takes a long time. That's why it doesn't happen often to people who break easily, or have sharp edges, or who have to be carefully kept. Generally, by the time you are Real, most of your hair has been loved off, and your eyes drop out and you get loose in your joints and very shabby. But these things don't matter at all, because once you are Real you can't be ugly, except to people who don't understand."

It takes sacrifice to make a difference. There is a cost to putting others first. But it is worth it!

Put Others First

I remember going to a committee meeting once when the chairman graciously offered to bring lunch for everyone. So, he stopped at the local deli and picked up his favorite sandwich for all-- Reuben sandwiches. Now I don't know about you, but my experience (including the experience of that meeting) has shown me that unless you live in the far north, most normal people do not like sauerkraut. Here is an example of someone, with great intentions, thinking more about what they liked instead of what others might like. A life-changing leader thinks first of the needs of others.

Recently, one of our coaches at the University of Mobile stopped me to say how blown away he was by the behavior of his boss who came over to him while he was working the door at a very busy game and offered to get him something to eat and drink. What a great example of putting the needs of others first and the impact it can make!

It is a simple concept called serving others. It is setting aside your needs and focusing on the needs of others. It is not expecting preferential treatment because you are the boss. Instead, it is offering preferential treatment to those you serve.

Motivate with Encouragement

I define encouragement as *using words to influence someone to be the best they can be*. This is not meaningless flattery. It is words that help people be their best. Let me stress, I am not talking about flattery. Flattery is using meaningless words to give others an unrealistic perspective.

I remember when I was in high school and it was youth Sunday at our church. I led the music and my closest friend (left unnamed here) preached the sermon. To say he struggled through his first preaching experience would be an understatement. Finally, when the service was over, we both stood at the back door and shook hands with the parishioners as they exited the sanctuary. Each person that passed by shook my friend's hand, telling him what a wonderful job he had done. I really wasn't sure they had been in the same service that I had been in. After a few more minutes of flattery, one man (actually, it was my dad) shook his hand and said, "I would think about selling insurance if I were you."

If you want to be an encourager, I really wouldn't advocate either approach as a general rule. If you can't find an honest word of encouragement in a situation like that, try saying something like, "Great effort!" That is still encouraging.

If you want to motivate those who work for you with encouraging words, they need to hear things like:

- *I really value you and the work you do*
- *I really appreciate how hard you work*
- *To me you represent what this company is all about*

Or, my favorite, when someone who works for me does something good:

- *I am so smart for hiring you!*

I love the scene in the movie *Braveheart* where William Wallace looks into the eyes of Robert the Bruce and tells him, "Men will follow courage and I see it in you! They will follow you. I will follow you!" You can see the eyes of Robert the Bruce light up with encouragement when he hears those words. When you believe in those who work for you, look them in the eyes and tell them.

There was a young man who played on my son's basketball team in Texas. He was not a particularly great basketball player, but I enjoyed watching him play because he played with an all-out attitude. I stopped him one day and said to him, "I really love the way you play. You play with great passion and I love that about you." After that, I would see him after other games and say things like, "Great defense," or "Great block!" It is interesting what began to happen. He would go out of his way to pass by me. He would come looking for me. You see, he was looking for encouragement. People will go out of their way to get encouraged.

I will never forget my sixth grade teacher, Mr. Rupp. My favorite part of school in the sixth grade was music. I loved music. I loved to sing. Every week he would pick a couple of students to come up to the front of the room and they would get to sing. In the course of the entire school year he never picked me once to sing in the front of the class. One day he called me to his desk and explained why I would never get a turn. He told me it was because I was a loser and I would never amount to anything. Now, maybe, he was trying to use some kind of reverse psychology on me in order to motivate me to be a better person. I really don't give him that much credit, but it doesn't matter because the approach is wrong no matter how you look at it. Those words were painful and devastating.

Contrast Mr. Rupp with my seventh grade music teacher, Mrs. White. The first week of school she told me I had a great voice and asked me to be in a special men's ensemble. She told me she wanted me to sit on the front row in choir class so my voice would stand out. I spent two years in her choirs and singing groups, had a lead in the eighth grade musical, and went on to be very involved in music in high school and college. I have since sung for movie stars, politicians, countless professional athletes, company presidents, multi-millionaires, college students, farmers, and everyday people from one end of the country to another. I have published songs, recorded albums and have had my songs recorded by other artists. I once even sang the national anthem for the Monday Night Game of the Week on national television. All I have to say about it all is, "Mr. Rupp, wherever you are, STICK IT IN YOUR EAR! Mrs. White, wherever you are, thanks for the encouragement and seeing the potential in me!"

Fuel Dreams

The great "theologian," Willy Wonka, once said, "We are the dreamers of dreams." Life-changing leaders help others dream dreams and find ways to fuel those dreams.

A couple of years ago a student from the university came by our house to hang out and talk. She was telling us about a dream she had. Someday she wanted her own business. It was fun listening to the excitement she had for her dream. When she graduated I bought her a book about successful women in business. I also put a one-dollar bill inside the book. When she opened it up, she said, "What is this for?" I told her that I wanted to be the first investor in her business, because I believed in her. Her face lit up!

I like to tell some folks, "I want to be president of your fan club! Just tell me where to send the t-shirts." Be president of somebody's fan club! Fuel those dreams. Be that kind of encourager.

Give Away Credit

Another very important way to motivate with encouragement is to give away credit. For some reason, many leaders are afraid to give away credit. I guess they feel others might not think they are doing a good job or their ego is so big that they demand all the credit. This is a real de-motivation to employees.

I once worked for a man whose motto was "protect the boss at all costs." He genuinely believed (and practiced) that all employees were expendable but the success of the company was solely contingent upon his success. Therefore everything was about making him look good. He encouraged his closest staff to always "take the hit" for any failures or shortcomings in the company so he could always lead from a position of success. In reality, that approach never made him a successful leader. He was only a successful loner. His approach was the opposite of how it should operate. A life-changing leader "takes the hit" for the people he or she leads.

When we have a meeting of our Board of Trustees, our division reports to a board committee. I love to review the highlights of our year with that committee and, in the presence of my staff, point out their individual leadership in making those things happen. Oh, I might have done many of those projects with them, but I want them to receive the credit. It motivates them and I really do value their work in a big way. Some might say, "If you give away the credit as a boss, you might make yourself expendable." An interesting sidelight of all of this is when my boss talks about me, he says, "He has the ability to put together an incredible team!" Giving away credit is always a win-win principle.

I read where, after every game, an All-Pro

running back in the NFL gives monetary gifts to his lineman equal to the amount of yards he gains. That is another great example of remembering to give credit where it is due.

Express Appreciation

I have a place in the top drawer of my desk where I keep notes people have sent me that really encourage me. They are the special notes, not the "Thanks, have a nice day, blah, blah, blah" notes. I am talking about the ones where someone sat down and thought through what they wanted to say and carefully crafted a meaningful message.

Every once and a while when I am having a rough day, I open up my top drawer and re-read some of those notes. They always encourage me! My goal is to always write "top drawer" notes to people. I challenge you to write meaningful notes of encouragement to those who work for you. Look for every opportunity to give out praise and encouragement.

Whenever someone on my staff has finished a big project, I like to give them a gift card for a meal or something fun. Most of the time I have no budget for it and I have to pay for it myself. But, it goes a long way to help them feel appreciated. It is worth the investment.

Pick up the tab at lunch. Pay for it out of your own pocket. Be generous. Express genuine appreciation.

Take Chances on People

Wilbur "Shooter" Flatch is a character played by Dennis Hopper in the movie *Hoosiers*. A former high school basketball hero, Flatch is now the town drunk. The basketball coach, played by Gene Hackman, decides to take a chance on Shooter and make him the assistant coach. At one point he even gets deliberately thrown out of the game so Shooter can have an opportunity to succeed. It is a tremendous illustration that reminds us to take chances on the "Shooters" in our lives.

When I was a sophomore in college, I had an opportunity to speak in a chapel service for the Kansas City Royals. The following week I met with a sportswriter from Detroit named Waddy Spoelstra.

At that time, Waddy was lining up speakers all by himself every Sunday in every major league city for chapel services. After we talked a while, he asked me if I would take care of all of the chapels in Kansas City. I said sure. Here I was, a young college student, and he was willing to take a chance on me working with major league athletes as the chaplain for the Royals. By the end of the season there were five of us helping Waddy in several cities across the country. Today there is a chaplain for every major league and minor league team in baseball.

Waddy took a chance on me, and I am better for it. Give people around you the opportunities to succeed. Take a chance.

Be Accessible

It is important to be available to those you lead. I have known bosses who always had their doors closed. That sends the wrong message. Keep your door open. Be available.

Every year, on student move-in day, I get to meet with the parents of the new incoming freshmen at our university. It is always a difficult day, especially for the moms, leaving their child to be on his or her own for the first time. I always close the meeting by giving the parents my cell phone number. That blows them away. They don't expect it. I want them to understand how committed we are to the best interests of their child. It is important they know that I am accessible to them.

Years ago, management guru Tom Peters introduced a concept called MBWA, or management by wandering around. I love this and practice it regularly. When I need to see someone on my staff, I will go to their office to meet with them. I love to get out and see what is working and who is doing great things.

Get out amongst your folks. Go to their offices. Stop by and see them. It shows that you are available to them and it helps you learn a lot about what is going on.

Empower for Success

Over the years I have observed two kinds of bosses. First, there are those who spend their time looking for policies to implement and rules to create for the people who work for them. Their favorite word is "no." Rules are what gives them their power. It is what makes them the boss. The other kind of boss—the kind who really makes a difference--is the one who spends time finding every way possible to help those he or she supervises experience real success.

I remember working for a guy who ended every staff meeting by saying "What can I do for you?" It was clear that he was genuinely interested in removing the obstacles that stood in the way of the success of those of us who worked for him. He wanted us to be our best and considered it his responsibility to see it happened. In the long run, this kind of leader has far more power—the power to help others be their absolute best.

Remove the Obstacles

If my job is to help my staff to be the best they can be, then I must know their needs and what I can do to help them. I don't ever like to leave a meeting or an encounter with a staff member without finding out those needs and any obstacles to their success. I view my responsibility as taking away the obstacles that keep them from being successful. How do you do that? Start with questions like these:

- What tools do you need?
- What roadblocks stand in your way?
- What can I do that would make your job easier?

I discovered one day that our soccer coach was frustrated. It was all because his scoreboard would not work. He was unable to focus on coaching soccer, because he was spending too much time trying to get it fixed. I told him to let me worry about the scoreboard. He needed to be coaching his players. It was a big burden off of his shoulders. I took care of it and he was able to spend his time doing what he does best.

Find out what is holding your folks back. Remove the obstacles. Help them succeed.

Go All the Way to the Dorm

If you are going to make a difference in someone's life and be an influence, then you have to go beyond the norm. You have got to do the extraordinary. It takes the extra.

I ran into a young lady in the hall of a classroom building the other day, and she was crying. So I put my arm around her shoulders and began to walk with her. She talked, and I talked, and before I knew it we were on the other side of the campus standing in front of the door to the dorm. Later she wrote me a note (I keep it in my top drawer). She wrote, "Mr. Blaylock, thanks for going all the way to the dorm with me." Going all the way to the dorm--I like that phrase. We need to go all the way to the dorm with folks if we want to make an impact in their lives.

One Sunday morning when I was in college, I was getting ready to go out and speak in a church in a little town out in Kansas. Before I headed for the car I was thumbing through my desk looking for something, and I found a surprise that I wasn't looking for. It was my phone bill. It was Sunday and the charges were due on Monday. The total bill was for $26.18. Well, the problem was that I had just taken all the money I had, all my quarters, all my change, everything, and put it in the gas tank of my car so I could get out to this church. So I prayed, "Lord, I'm going to have to depend on you to help me with that phone bill." I grabbed my Bible and headed for the car.

I got to the church and the pastor met me at the door. He thanked me for coming and told me that during the service they were going to take a love offering for me to help with my expenses. I thanked him while trying to hide my excitement and silently reminded God about the phone bill.

After the service I was standing at the back door shaking hands with people as they come out. The last person out the door was the chairman of the deacons. He shook my hand and slapped a wad of bills in my hand and said, "Mike, this is the money that was in the offering plate this morning. We hope it helps you out with your expenses." It was a total of $26.16.

Now, you remember the phone bill is $26.18. That's two cents short. Well, you know every once in a while you'll find a penny lying on the ground? I walked around all day looking for pennies. I wound up borrowing a couple of cents from my roommate, and the next morning I paid the phone bill.

And so I got to thinking, what's the lesson from that story? Is it that we need to give our two cents' worth? No, that's too corny. Actually, that is not the answer, it is the problem. Too many times all we give is two cents' worth of our lives. Two cents' worth of effort; two cents' worth of care; two cents' worth of time--and we're always expecting the $26.18 to just happen. We have to give our all, not two cents' worth.

Give others your all! Go all the way to the dorm!

Demonstrate Character

On a cold Tuesday night in November 2002, I sat in the stands at a park in Bowling Green, Kentucky and watched our men's soccer team from the University of Mobile win the NAIA National Championship. It was awesome! I have been to a World Series and several American League Championship Playoffs while chaplain for the Kansas City Royals. I have had the experience of being on the winning side of a bowl game while chaplain for the University of Tulsa football team and coached a high school team to a three-state championship. But, all of these combined cannot touch the excitement I shared with these young men and their championship. This was particularly special because of what I witnessed in the lives of these athletes.

The head coach made some deliberate roster moves in the off-season in order to improve the character of his team and began the season with a new, strict, no bad-language policy. Any use of inappropriate language would result in the dreaded and gut-wrenching national wind sprint drill. It only took a couple of incidents early in the first week to curb the excess verbage. Now, I know it may seem odd that there was a need for a no-cussing rule at a Christian university. Understand, not every student who attends a Christian university is a Christian. In fact, many of these soccer players came from all around the world and experienced some adjustments in the Christian environment.

I saw these and other influences begin to transform individuals and, ultimately, the team. Guys would walk away from situations on the field instead of jumping right in the middle of trouble. Others who had played only for themselves became very unselfish. As it turned out, what had been 35 penalty violations for language and attitude during the previous season became one solitary call that the referee later admitted was a mistake this year. In 30 years of working with athletes on all levels, I have never seen such a complete transformation of character on a team as with this one. Ultimately, I believe that it was their character that led them to win the national championship. And, for me, it was watching that character develop in the lives of a group of athletes that I came to love that made that championship so uniquely special and rewarding.

  Character is critical for a life-changing leader. Those you lead must see you as genuine. You cannot be one thing in private and something different in front of everyone. Like my soccer players, you must make a commitment to be consistent in your behavior. If you make a mistake, admit it and move on.

  The example of corporate and political leadership the past few years in our country has been disheartening. If those leaders had followed one simple rule, it would have made all the difference. If you and I would simply follow this rule we will be a great example of life-changing character to those we lead. <u>Always do what is right</u>. Whatever situation you face, no matter what it costs, no matter where you wind up--always do what is right. You will make a difference.

See the Big Picture

A life-changing leader has perspective. One of my first bosses called it "being an anticipator." It is seeing the big picture and how everyone fits into it. It is looking beyond every decision and knowing what will come next. It is understanding what really matters in the long term.

I remember visiting my aunt when I was young and helping her put together a jigsaw puzzle. It was not one of those puzzles for kids, but a serious puzzle with what seemed like a million pieces. It was hard to imagine we would ever get it put together. It was difficult to figure out what went where because so many pieces looked the same. Fortunately, there was a picture on the box of what the puzzle was supposed to look like when it was put together. When you looked at the picture, it helped you see where the puzzle piece fit in. Perspective is seeing the picture on the box and understanding how the pieces fit together because you know what it is supposed to look like. It is knowing that the pieces are very small in comparison to the picture.

The Small Pieces

The small pieces of the puzzle are those things that are a part of putting the picture together, but they are not the big picture itself. It is easy to lose perspective when these small pieces are all so different. Perhaps the most overemphasized small pieces in life are winning and losing.

Former University of North Carolina coach Dean Smith has won more college basketball games than nearly any other coach in history. He expressed his perspective when he said, "If you make every game a life-and-death proposition . . . you'll be dead a lot." Coach Smith understands that winning and losing are small pieces. Successful coaches know that life is bigger than the outcome of the game.

Terry had never played organized baseball in his life when he came out for the team I was coaching his senior year in high school. He had very little ability but a lot of heart and was a great kid. Since we only had ten other guys go out for the team, I let him suit up and gave him a spot on the team. For the entire season he kept the scorebook, hauled the water jug and helped with the equipment, but never actually played. Near the end of the season, we traveled to a nearby town to play a small school with an excellent program. Two of my starters were competing in a school-sponsored math contest. So, the inevitable happened. I had to play Terry.

After looking over the roster I decided the only place I could play him was at first base. The game was a pitching duel and remained scoreless until the fifth inning. Our pitcher walked a man who ultimately wound up on second. With two outs the next batter hit a slow grounder to first. Terry, in good fielding position, reached down to scoop up the ball, only to have it roll through his legs and into the outfield. The runner scored and we went on to lose the game 1-0.

During the bus ride home, I was concerned that Terry might be taking the loss hard, so I went back to where he was and sat down next to him. I put my arm on his shoulder and said, "Terry, you did a great job! Don't let one error bother you." He looked up at me and said, "I am not upset at all, coach!" A bit surprised by his response (I wanted him to be a little upset), I asked him why he wasn't upset at all. He replied, "Coach, I got to play!"

Terry's perspective on the game was bigger than mine. I was looking at the outcome and he was looking at how playing in that game fit into his life. For him, the experience of the game was worth it all. Too many of us go through life worried about the score and miss the blessing of just being in the game.

Marv Levy coached the Buffalo Bills to four Super Bowls and lost all four. When a reporter asked how he handled it, he said, "I'd rather get to this level and lose than be sitting home watching." That is perspective.

If you are going to be a life-changing leader, you must be able to distinguish between the small pieces and the picture on the box. That means looking beyond wins, losses, recognition and disappointment. Perspective is seeing what's really important and not losing sight of it.

The Picture on the Box

If you as a leader are to help others succeed, you must understand the definition of real success. Real success is not winning games, gaining recognition, or reaching goals. Real success is being the best you can be. It's reaching and maintaining your maximum potential. You will accomplish that in your own life as you help others to be the best they can be. Great coaches understand that principle.

I have a good friend who is one of the most successful high school football coaches in the state of Oklahoma. When I asked him what the ultimate goal of coaching is for him, he said it is to help boys become men.

Former Nebraska football coach Tom Osborne's philosophy of coaching placed a strong emphasis on the personal development of his players. In his book, *More Than Winning*, he explains five characteristics he tried to emphasize in their lives. He wanted his players to be disciplined, to learn to be the best they can be, to develop perseverance, to have a broadened experience and to develop spiritual awareness or commitment.

For Coach Osborne, success was measured by what was accomplished in the lives of his players. That was his big picture. He placed his emphasis on helping his players be all they could be.

Lou Holtz understands that life is bigger than football. In his book, *Winning Every Day*, he explains one of those important lessons.

As I told our football team on those occasions when things are going against us: "Don't get discouraged. Someday, you are going to be thirty-one years old with three or four kids. One day you'll wake up to discover that the bank has just foreclosed on your mortgage and that your wife has just run off with some drummer. But you won't blink an eye, because what we're encountering now is teaching you how to survive hard times. Handling adversity is part of life.

The big picture has to do with life. It is knowing that life is bigger than the small pieces. For the leader, it's helping others to be the best they can be. Sometimes that involves winning and other times it involves losing. When the puzzle is finally put together, it is a picture of real success.

How Do You Get Perspective?

Perspective is not something you gain from reading a book or going to a seminar. It comes from paying attention to life. You get perspective by learning from three key areas. You must learn from failures, learn from victories and learn from time.

Learn from Failures

The successful leader knows that mistakes, losses and disappointments are learning experiences. Failure is a great teacher. It teaches us perspective. Baseball is a game of perspective. A ballplayer is considered great if he hits over .300, but that means seven out of ten times he failed to hit the ball. Hall of Famer Mickey Mantle once pointed out that during his 18 years in the major leagues he came to bat almost 8,400 times. He had a total of 2,474 career hits. Averaging around 500 at bats a season, it means he played the equivalent of twelve years without even hitting the ball. Failures are a part of life, they go hand in hand with success.

NFL coaching great Don Shula's favorite saying is "Success is not forever, and failure isn't fatal." I would say that failure is only fatal when we fail to see it as a small piece of the puzzle. Failure is not a terrible thing; failure to learn from failure is. In proper perspective, failure is the teacher that leads you to success. Learn from your failures and losses. They will teach you perspective.

Learn from Victories

What do victories teach us? We learn they are small pieces because they are short-lived. Trophies tarnish and newspaper headlines change every day. It is a short trip from the cover of *Sports Illustrated* to obscurity. Rick Pitino led the University of Kentucky to the NCAA championship in 1996. He understands that championships and victories fade quickly. Pitino writes in his book, *Success is a Choice*,

> Success can be a minefield, full of hidden obstacles and booby traps just waiting to trip you up. Success never comes sugar-coated with guarantees of longevity. A few missteps, a few moments of letting down your guard—this is a poisonous pill that, if swallowed, can turn long-striven-for success into overnight failure.

How does it happen? It happens when you embrace success itself and forget the work it took to get you there.

Hall of Famer Frank Robinson observed, "When a club wins, it is difficult the next year to get the players to dedicate themselves the way they did before. The players aren't as hungry the next year."

If success is measured by a single accomplishment, then it is over as soon as it happens. Any coach or athlete who wins a championship knows that the satisfaction of that win fades quickly. Like Pitino and Robinson, they also understand that a new season is just around the bend and success has to happen all over again. Winston Churchill once said, "Success is never final." It is important to remember that success is a journey—not a destination. It's being all you can be all the time, and that's not over until you breathe your last breath.

Learn from Time

Mark was the ace pitcher on the high school baseball team I coached. He had pretty good stuff, but his biggest weakness was that he tended to be a bit overconfident at times. We were playing in the finals of the Beggs, Oklahoma Invitational Tournament against a team from a nearby town, and Mark was the starting pitcher. He was really excited because there were several college coaches and a number of folks from the media there to watch a player on the other team. He felt that this was his big chance to show what he could do. Early in the game he found himself pitching to the young man everyone had come to see. Mark decided to throw him his best fastball, just to prove how good he was, so he rared back and hummed it in there. Well, all I remember seeing was our centerfielder watch the ball soar over the fence. After that, Mark fell apart, gave up several more runs before coming out of the game. He was devastated. His chance to prove himself had turned to disaster. You know, for quite some time you couldn't even get him to talk about it. It had been the worst day in his life. However, it's amazing how perspective changes things. If you asked him about that game now, he would gladly tell you the story. It is now one of the great moments of his life. That's because the player from the other team who hit the homerun eventually gave up baseball and went on to lead the Dallas Cowboys to the Super Bowl . . . Troy Aikman.

It's amazing how time makes everything look different. The real picture looks a lot different when you mix it with time.

Legendary coach Amos Alonzo Stagg, when asked one year if he felt his season was a success, replied, "I'll tell you in about fifteen years." He believed that only time would reveal if his players were successful because their success had more to do with the outcome of their lives. That is the perspective necessary to be a life-changing leader.

Prevent People Problems

Over the years I have wanted to write a leadership book and call one chapter "Get Rid of the Idiots." Anyone who has been in a leadership position will relate to the frustration of working with people who simply did not belong where they were. Somewhere, someone thought they had potential to be successful and promoted them to a position of leadership. Instead, they became a hindrance to the organization and a problem that someone eventually had to clean up. The answer I want to provide for getting rid of the idiots is preventative. It happens by learning to find the right people for your organization.

Phil Savage is a very successful "finder of right people." His success has led him to be the General Manager of the Cleveland Browns. As Director of Scouting and later Director of Player Personnel for the Baltimore Ravens, he helped lead the Ravens to draft more athletes that have "made it" in the NFL than any other team. A part of this success Phil credits to a simple matrix that rates players according to three essential characteristics. Over time he has discovered that all of the players who succeeded possessed the same three characteristics on his matrix. Those they drafted who did not succeed were missing at least two of the three. Those essential characteristics combined with talent became "must haves" for every player they drafted.

Now you are wondering, "What are the three magical characteristics?" Actually the characteristics for contributing to a NFL football team are not the same as those that predict success in your business. The characteristics are not the point—the point is the matrix. You must identify those essentials for success in your business and plug them into your own matrix for finding the right person. Look at the employees in your organization who are making it happen. What do they have in common? Which characteristics stand out as "magical" for you? Make them your organization's "must haves" and then nurture those characteristics.

Great sports teams usually have a distinguishing characteristic. Rick Pitino's college basketball teams always have had an "in your face" style of play. The Los Angeles Lakers in the NBA made the term "Showtime" famous. The NFL's Raiders have always been known for their tenacious defense. The Larry Bird-era Boston Celtics stood out with a hard-working "blue collar" image. In every case those teams looked for players who fit that style or image and were successful. The same is true for you.

Learn to Inspire

A life-changing leader inspires others to be the best they can be. Coaches understand this important principle. Herb Brooks was the coach of the legendary 1980 U.S. Olympic Hockey Team. Before the semifinal game with the heavily favored Russians, he walked into the locker room and spoke to his players. He simply said, "You were born to be hockey players. You were meant to be here. This is your night." That night the Americans made history beating the "unbeatable" Russians. The words of Coach Brooks are considered to be one of the greatest sports motivational speeches ever.

No one could ever accuse Tommy Lasorda of lacking emotion. He defines an important characteristic found in successful leaders: passion. His enthusiasm and love for the game were his trademarks as manager of the Los Angeles Dodgers baseball team for twenty years, leading the team to World Series titles in 1981 and 1988. In his book, *Out of the Blue*, pitcher Orel Hershiser tells of a meeting he had with Lasorda early in his rookie year that turned his career around. Lasorda would later call it his "Sermon on the Mound." The manager sat Hershiser down and at a fever pitch said,

You don't believe in yourself! You are scared to pitch in the big leagues! Who do you think these hitters are, Babe Ruth? Ruth's dead! You got good stuff. If you didn't, I wouldn't have brought you up. Quit being so careful! Go after the hitter . . . If I could get a heart surgeon in here, I'd have him take out my heart, open your chest and take out your heart, and then I'd have him give you my heart. You'd be in the Hall of Fame! If I had your stuff, I'd'a been in the Hall of Fame!

I've seen guys come and go, son, and you've got it! You gotta go out there and do it on the mound! Take charge! Make 'em hit your best stuff! Be aggressive. Be a bulldog out there. That's gonna be your new name: Bulldog. You know, when we bring you in the ninth to face Dale Murphy and he hears, 'Now pitching, Orel Hershiser,' man, he can't wait till you get there! But if he hears, 'Now pitching, Bulldog Hershiser,' he's thinkin', Oh, no, who's that!? Murphy's gonna be scared to death!

Lasorda's passion motivated Orel Hershiser to success. He went on to win the Cy Young Award, earn MVP honors in both the playoffs and the World Series, lead his team to the championship and was named *Sports Illustrated's* Sportsman of the Year, all in one season.

Like Tommy Lasorda, life-changing leaders inspire others to great success. They make a difference. Be a student of inspirational leaders.

Read books about them. Hang out with them. Learn how to inspire people to great things!

Focus on What is Important

The psalmist prayed that God would remind him that our time here is brief and life is fleeing away (Psalm 39:4). I believe he needed that reminder because he wanted to always remember to stay focused on what is most important. The truth is that we all are dying and every day is precious. Our lives need to stay focused on a greater purpose. I want to spend my days making a difference in the lives of those around me. What about you? What is important to you?

When I was diagnosed with cancer it changed my perspective on a lot of things. I began to plan out my week asking the question, "If this was my last week, what would I want to get done before it's over?" With all apologies to Tim McGraw, nothing on my list had anything to do with sky diving or riding a bull named Fu Manchu. It was all about people. I set up my schedule meeting with people I wanted to influence. None of us should have to get cancer to feel the urgency of helping others be the best they can be. It should be what is most important. When my days on this earth are finished, I want one phrase written on my tombstone: He made a difference.

Make people the priority in your schedule. Get fired up about them. Focus on their needs. Help them to be the best they can be. Whatever it costs you, make the sacrifice. Inspire, fuel dreams. Be an encourager. In doing so, you will find fulfillment in what you do. You will be a life-changing leader.

Epilogue

There are those who say that you cannot always have the best interests of your employees in mind and still have a successful company. I say that depends on your definition of success. If your goal is to make as much money as fast as you can or to climb to the top in record time, you will not be interested in the principles of life-changing leadership. But there is so much more. I believe that real success is making your life count. It is finding fulfillment in being the absolute best you can be. It is serving others.

I once worked for a boss who imposed his success-at-all-cost leadership style on me. Therefore, I found myself using fear and intimidation to squeeze the absolute most out of our employees. Whenever they quit producing, they were replaced. I finally came to a place in my life where that approach just wasn't worth it, and I never want to be in that kind of position again. If you have reached a place of seasoning or maturity in your life where fulfillment is worth more than money or status, life-changing leadership is for you. You get it. Take it and run with it.

I would be remiss if I did not tell you that these principles of life-changing leadership have been developed from a personal study of the greatest leader of all time, Jesus Christ. Over a period of several years I examined the gospels of Matthew, Mark, Luke and John to learn how Jesus dealt with people. I looked closely at his relationships with others and the methods he employed to make them their best. They are tried and true and have been proven successful. No one has influenced more people than Jesus Christ. He changed my life.

I encourage you to do your own study of his life and principles. Learn from his example. It is what life-changing leadership is all about.